GUIDE FOR THE NEXT GIRL

Guide for the Next Girl

Printed in the United States of America
ISBN-13: 979-8-218-26308-9

GUIDE FOR THE NEXT GIRL

The girl you were doesn't have to be the girl
you'll become.

DAZEJAH MAE

To the girl who wants to leave a legacy in the world,
and who desires to find someone who can relate,
this book is for you.

CONTENTS

BONUS CONTENT

Introduction

Even as a little girl, I've always had big dreams from wanting to be a teacher, to being a business owner, to a dance teacher, I have always been a dreamer. And now that I'm older I still am a huge dreamer but I'm also a realist. I believe what is the point of following our dreaming if we don't make a plan to get there. I wanted to start this chapter by talking about what I would have told my younger self. And I hope that you learn something new and can apply some of the advice that I share.

BE MORE OPEN

I would have told myself that it is okay to be more open about how I feel about something and to voice my opinion more. And that it is okay that you can't control what others think about you or how others perceive you. So go talk to that boy, go make that new friend, and go ride that roller coaster because in the end, one day you'll regret that you didn't. And the worst thing you can do is be on your deathbed, full of regret for all the things you wish you did but didn't. And that you could have been known but hid.

SAY NO MORE

You don't always have to say yes, I wasn't put on this planet to please man and do whatever others call me to do. It is okay if now that I say no when someone asks me to do something that is outside of my boundaries, I'm not comfortable with, and when I simply just don't want to do it. I have the right to say no.

And by saying no more I'm now able to give my future self what my younger self didn't get, which is the ability to be myself and do all the things I am called to do and dream of without fear of rejection from those who feel I'm just their puppet.

KEEP MORE THINGS TO YOURSELF

You do not have to tell everyone your business, not everyone needs to know your goals, your dreams, and what's going on in your life. Although we shouldn't keep everything to ourselves, we need people on our side cheering for us, some people want to know your business, and it's not for the right reasons. One of my favorite quotes is **what people don't know, they can't ruin.**

REMEMBER EVERYONE HAS FEELINGS

Everyone has feelings even if they don't always show them. And I have learned that there is life and death in the tongue and even though that person may not show their feelings often or seem like they are always fine, we all have good days and bad days. And that mean girl who is so rude to you and doesn't seem to care about your feelings, the truth is she does and even if it is behind closed doors she is struggling too. So always be kind, smile at everyone, and be real about how you are feeling because maybe others will open up too.

IT IS NEVER TOO LATE UNTIL IT'S TOO LATE

It is never too late until it is, we have numbered days that we are here on this Earth, and the thing is we never know how long. So if you have been dreaming of doing something whether that is traveling, talking to a certain person, going to the gym, or trying a new hobby My advice is DO IT, you won't regret it. I started playing a sport my senior year of high school and I look back now, and I had too much fun, and I learned so much and it is now too late for me to go back and get involved in more sports or have started my sport earlier. So, in response to that, go do what you long for, you won't regret it.

XOXO,
Dazejah Mae

Chapter 1

Life

"Live life to the fullest because you only get one"

Your story isn't over. We were all made for a time such as this, God fearfully and wonderfully made us, He knitted us together in the womb and chose you and I to be alive in this generation.

And then we were born into a fallen world with sin and pain and life isn't always fun and we will go through trials and heartache **but HERE IS SOME GOOD NEWS.... Your STORY ISNT OVER YET.** Jesus overcame the grave and bore your sins on the cross over 2,000 years ago and there is nothing Satan can do to defeat what God has planned for you. Your story isn't over. Life is something we all have, and we all go through, and if it's something we all go through, Why does it hurt so much sometimes? Why do some people go through such a hard and painful life and others seem to go through the life we long for?

And these might be some thoughts you think about and wonder about every day but as your big sister, I'm obligated to share some truth with you to help you see life in a different light.

One of my favorite sayings is **simply being alive is completely different than living.** When you're alive you're breathing and functioning but when you are living, you're saying that I get one life, and my life is worth it and I'm going to make the most of my time here on earth. And even when times get hard you still see life as one to live.

One thing I believe helps us get through life more smoothly is Journaling our thoughts, emotions, and our daily life. Having one journal that only you can see, only you can use, and only you can be you to the fullest. So yes, life can be hard but that doesn't mean it isn't worth it, and you are worth it, so live.

LETTING SOMEONE GO

One of the hardest things we have to do on this earth is to let someone go willingly, letting go of a situation that you were in and if were being honest it is so hard to do but sometimes so necessary. And when we have to let people go it can be one of the best things we could do, yes let me repeat that **LETTING THE WRONG PEOPLE GO IS ONE OF THE BEST THINGS YOU COULD DO.** And, let me elaborate when God closes doors for us and He always opens new ones in His timing. And don't forget God also hears conversations that you didn't and if the situation isn't good for you and you won't remove them, then He will but that's something worth praising for.

GOING THROUGH SEASONS

The honest reality is that to get a rainbow, rain must come. In other words, for change to occur in we must go through seasons before we see what we have been waiting for. And there are all sorts of seasons from seasons of singleness, seasons of loneliness, seasons of heartbreak. And the other side of those seasons would include a relationship, genuine friendships, or healing.

And Ecclesiastes 3:1 says "For everything there is a season." This just shows that there is a time for everything and when one season ends that means that another one will begin. This is why it is so important to enjoy each season, whether it's a hard season or one of the best seasons of your life. You never know when or if you'll get another like it.

Each season teaches us a lesson and we can take something from each one, and when the season ends, we can rejoice in the fact that we got to experience that Season of opportunity because every season teaches us something.

PERSEVERING THROUGH THE TOUGH TIMES

Sister, things are going to get hard because of the type of world we live in. One of my guy friends said something that struck me, he said "God loved Jesus and he still suffered." And because we are on this earth and because there is sin, there is always going to be suffering because hurt people hurt people. And no one on this Earth is exempt from pain and suffering.

And that doesn't mean we accept people mistreating us, but we can remind ourselves that with pain there is also hope and healing on the other side. And yes, things are going to get hard but when they do, we can hold fast to the idea that pain is temporary, and the season won't last forever and there are people who love you.

And when times get really hard and you feel like you can't make it through remember that God is able, and He wants you to give your burdens to him. And that there are people who want to walk alongside you when times get hard and be a shoulder you can cry on and vent to. So, when you feel at your lowest, don't give up on your tribe, they got your back. And finally, don't give up, you are loved and worthy and you were chosen to be here, you are stronger than you think you are.

FAMILY

I want you to listen closely, where you came from doesn't define you. Your family doesn't define you, how you were treated doesn't define you, what you were called doesn't define you. What truly matters is how you spend your life moving forward. Are you going to be a generational curse breaker? Are you going to make a difference?

That's what matters, not where you came from, it is about the heart. And in life, we don't get to choose who our families are, but we do get to choose who and what we call family moving forward as we get older.

GUIDE PUT TO ACTION

VERSE TO MEMORIZE:

"Blessed is the one who preserves under trail because, having stood the test, that person will receive the crown of life that the Lord has promised to those who love him."

James 1:12

ACTION:

+ Use your time wisely so go Volunteer, Start a Small Group, or Start a new hobby (don't waste this season!)
+ Write down your story of your life so far, all the good, bad, and ugly
+ Journal how your dream life, everything from your ideal friendships, relationships, and career

MY TIP TO YOU:

+ Write letters to people who hurt you or write down how much that situation hurt you on a plate and then break it, Write down your fears on balloon and let it go, (Do What you gotta do to let it go.

APPLICATION:

+ Start a journal and journal each day to see how far you have come
+ Create a Bucket List of everything that you want to do in this life & Start Living it

Last thoughts:

Life is a beautiful thing, and it won't always be easy but it will be worth it in the end. So, enjoy this one life that you have and make it count and one worth remembering.

Chapter 2

Boys

"With the right guy, all you will have to do is exist."

First things first, let me tell you a story from my life. It all started in middle school (such a throwback, haha). Okay so in middle school I had the biggest crush on a guy…and I did the worst thing, which was chase him, even though I knew he did not like me. (Ladies don't do this)

And I even put on a bunch of makeup and posted a zillion insta stories just so he would see it (do not do this). And then after wasting my summer having a huge crush on him, something happened (yes, my precious summer, I don't know why I was so native).

All of a sudden, I had the strangest but most blessed realization the miracle one, that is from God. And all of a sudden, I just stopped liking him and I realized that I have been putting my worth in how he felt about me, and I instant realized I had to leave, and I know that sounds crazy, but It changed everything for me.

And I know what you may be thinking about how this exactly relates to this chapter, I'll tell you. This shows how we get so caught up in a guy sometimes that we miss living the moment, and when a guy shows us by his actions that he doesn't want us, we turn a blind eye anyways because it's our way or the highway and even though many times I should have let go, I didn't until a divine intervention happened.

And, now to get into the chapter what you're probably thinking why not worry about guys and why do we have to talk about guys, because you already know so much about them. And girl I've been there trust me what I wish someone would have told me that being attracted to guys your age is okay and liking them is okay too. But (and yes there is always a but) there is a consequence to the boy crazy phase. First things first you lose yourself one way or another in the process.

Okay let's get back to the basics, First in the Boy Craze phase, when your Boy Crazy several things can happen but first let me define boy crazy: **extremely enthusiastic about boys and the definition for eustatically. Intense, interest, and approval.** Did you see the pattern? 'intense' and 'approval' that we as ladies that are showing boys instead of ourselves and if you're reading this and you're probably either in junior high, high school, or college and have been there, now let's get into it a little more.

Okay so if you ask someone why we get boy crazy one of the number one things they'll say is hormones but let's talk about other cases as well if you lack self-confidence, or you're very codependent, or if you simply love male validation, they can have a bigger impact for you to be boy crazy and guys will pray on that. If a guy sees that you love his attention and he knows that he can get you at any time, then as your big sister I'm obligated to tell you that he will take advantage of you and I'm saying this because I love you through the screen. DISCLAIMER: I'M NOT SAYING ALL GUYS ARE LIKE THIS, BUT IMMATURE BOYS ARE. I DON'T WANT YOU TO GO THROUGH THAT.

One of the biggest pieces of advice that I can give you is to let a guy pursue and chase you when the time is right and when it's meant to happen, your prince charming will find you. And until then girl I'm telling you not to worry about seeing your friends in relationships, and maybe even seeing other people around you are getting what you feel you deserve, just wait.

Other things you could do instead of waiting is learn more about yourself and what you love to do and live your life to the fullest, maybe it's making new and genuine friendships, finding your passions, or learning a new skill. A wise person once told me that "the process will take as long as you allow it to take" In other words if you want to be the person you always wanted to be *then work on it (especially while you're single).*

You can work on your body, instead of waiting years to put in the work and complaining about it, put in the work now, and within a few months, you'll see the changes. Maybe you want to get all A's or good grades this semester *(for my college gals!)* and then if that's you work hard and study now and within weeks it'll make a difference and you'll see a change from your hard work.

Let's talk about knowing if a guy is the one or not based on the boundaries he may or may cross and his actions towards you.

First, let's clear up a few things to look out for in a guy to discern if he is or is not the one:

- He pressures you to move to second base when you're not comfortable
- He gives you ultimatums like if you don't move to second base then he will break up with you
- He wants to get physical within first meeting you(Runnn)

Those are **some huge red flags** in guys, I'll say this so many times in this book, but it is so powerful, if he respects you, he will wait, and he won't even put you in that position in the first place. If he, does you simply know where he stands, a real guy will treat you the way you deserve to be treated.

Now let's get into green flags to know if he is the one for you

- He holds open the door whether it is your car door or the door of the restaurant he's a gentleman
- He respects your parents (if he meets them), and he will use words like ''Ma'am'' and ''Sir'' with your parents (husband material sis!)
- He respects your boundaries and doesn't make multiple attempts to cross them (he also sets boundaries)
- He talks to you with respect he doesn't degrade you (he builds you up with his words, not tears you down)
- He is the same guy in front of you and with others (he is being himself and not putting up a front)
- He talks about you in a good light in front of his friends, he

doesn't try and degrade your reputation(talk more about this in a later chapter)

Now, let's talk about some boundaries we can set to help us further better our relationships with guys

- Leave him on delivered sometimes (make him wait to get your response)
- Don't give in too easily, make him chase you (As Queen Alexa Cappelli said, ''I'll only chase if there's somewhere to run)
- **Set clear expectations** ("I'm not okay with going to second base")
- **Let him pursue you** (if he's interested in you, he will make an effort)
- **Talk about your goals and expectations for the relationship** (''I don't want to do...." Or ''I would love to do....")

It's so important to understand how a guy treats you, especially in the beginning, his initiatives are how he feels about you, if a guy is putting in the effort to get to know you and genuinely cares about you, will know. Now having that said as well if he doesn't respect you, will know by his actions towards you. Now it is also important to realize that some guys aren't as respectful as you are when it comes to what happens between you guys behind the scenes.

Storytime, it was Springtime, and I was on the bus and there was this guy who always sat behind me. This guy was talking to his friends about his girlfriend (who wasn't on the bus and went to another school) and the private things they did and the results of that out loud, he told their private business and exposed it. Maybe he didn't mean it to hurt her, and I don't think she knew he told others about it and maybe he had loved her, but he didn't respect her enough to keep what they did privately between them.

Now the reason I'm telling you this is because it's important to choose a guy who is going to not only love you **but respect you, the way you deserve in front of you and when you're not around.**

GUIDE PUT TO ACTION

VERSE TO MEMORIZE:

"The man who finds a wife finds a treasure and receives favor from the Lord."

Proverbs 18:22

ACTION:

+ Create a list of some boundaries you have and work towards putting up boundaries with the guys in your life

MY TIP TO YOU:

+ Never chase a guy no Matter how much you like him. Countless of guys have said they like the chase, so let them chase.

APPLICATION:

+ Start a journal and journal each day to see how far you have come
+ Apply what you learned and create your own green, yellow, and red flag list

Last thoughts:

Never be desperate for a guy's attention,
they know and will be less interested.

Chapter 3

Friendships

"No one can be your everything, but everyone have something to say, something to teach you, and something to bring joy in your life."

—JENNIE ALLEN

When you hear the word friendship what do you think about? Do you think about how you don't have any really good friendships? How you are satisfied with the friendships you have right now? Or how you long for genuine raw healthy friendships? The reality is that we all have different thoughts surrounding friendships and we should bring back having conversations about our feelings in regards to friends. In our life we all have these people: our coworkers, our teammates, our classmates, and our neighbors. But are they really our friends or are they more of just our acquaintances that are meant to be in our lives for the time being?

Let me tell you a story, I was on one of the sports teams I did in high school. And I remember my coach at the time asked us all to get into groups of 3 and we had about 20 girls on our team, and I remember turning around and everyone was getting into groups and not one person asked me to be in their group. If I could only describe how that affected me, the feeling of being left out.

And I know that these girls were like a family to me but the feelings I felt of being left out, words I couldn't even describe. All I could remember is going home and crying to my mom and I cried a lot that night because I felt that feeling a little bit too much. And as I mentioned before I also write songs and I remember feeling like I had all of these people around me and yet I felt so alone, and I wrote some good songs from that time in my life.

And the reason I'm telling you that story is in hopes of showing how in life you are going to go through periods in your life when you have tons of great friends and other periods where you are in the waiting period of waiting for that God-Given community for your life and that sometimes you'll have to be alone to grow and when that one day comes you'll see why you went through that season.

Another piece of advice when it comes to friendships in general that I believe can be such a hard thing to accept is the fact of temporary friendships. I feel like it's common sense to know that every person we will meet won't be in our life forever, but I believe the fact of truly accepting that can be hard. I had a best friend that I met in preschool, and we were best friends until the end of elementary and I thought our friendship would be a forever friendship, but we went to different schools and became too busy for each other. And there was the end of our friendship, and I believe that taught me was to be grateful for the memories you had with each friend and to cherish every moment like it's your last.

And as I moved through middle school, I hung out with a group of girls that I thought were my friends, and boy was I wrong. I was friends with girls who were jealous of me, didn't respect me as a person, and talked behind my back. And despite all of the red flags right in front of my face, I accepted the bare minimum of these girls, and when they showed me who they were by excluding me from the group and not inviting me to things and telling other things I told them in confidence I just couldn't see what was in front of my face until I could. And all along my mom could see it, and I'm sure others could as well. And the reason I'm telling this story from my life is because as I talked about not accepting the bare minimum from a boy, also applies to not accepting the bare minimum from a friend.

Let me elaborate when I talk about not accepting the bare minimum from a friend. We all have different levels we associate our friends with. One friend we deem as our best friend, another friend we deem as a close friend, and maybe another as just a friend. But I may add that, a friend does the same thing to you and has you deemed. To you, that friend may be your best friend and to them, you're just a close friend. One way you can know what they deem you as is by their actions and efforts towards you. But also, by simply asking them, 'What am I to you?" or "What do you consider me as."

Now once you know what you are to that person set expectations within that friendship. First by simply stating what you will and will not accept like you would in a relationship. That you will not accept peer pressure, rude comments about your appearance, etc. Knowing your worth completely out weights what others think about you. You want raw genuine friendships of people who will be there through the sun and stay during the storm.

Lastly, to conclude about friendships is that life can be hard, but it can also be joyful, and I truly believe we were meant to need each other. I encourage you to find people who will be your rock and be there when you need it, but a step further I aspire you to be that for someone else. We all go through silent battles, that we fake a smile just so others don't see the pain that we are facing. So, in response to that text a friend and ask how their mental health is, how it is going at home, and how's school going. Because we need people who look out for us, but it can't be one-sided.

Praying and hoping you find your people and you reciprocate that forward!

GUIDE PUT TO ACTION

VERSE TO MEMORIZE:

"As iron sharpens iron, so one person sharpens another."

Proverbs 27:17

ACTION:

+ Write down what you would consider and ideal friend and then work on being that friend that you want

MY TIP TO YOU:

+ Not everyone is going to be your friend or like you and that is okay. Learn to accept acquaintances so just continue to be yourself

APPLICATION:

+ Start a journal and journal each day to see how far you have come
+ Create a list of all your friends & Select 3 or 4 you want to prioritize and pour into and then do just that

Last thoughts:

Seek out community in whatever season you are in, we need each other!

Chapter 4

Power of Influence

*"Never Underestimate the influence that
you have on others"*

—LAURIE BUCHANAN

Influence. One word with a lot of power. The power to change the world or make the world worse. The definition is **have an influence on** and it's a verb. I believe there is power in influence and the truth is we've all been influenced since birth. Since we were younger, we've watched other people, especially our parents, we observed and imitated them.

Have you seen a parent do something and then the child does the exact same thing, that's observational learning. Have you ever watched someone do something that inspired you and then you did it, that's observational learning. The truth is we all have been influenced and have influenced others and there is power in that.

One thing I'm very passionate about is influencing other people. We all have influenced someone whether it was in a good way or bad way. And one of my favorite sayings is **if you know better, then do better.** And I believe that's something we should all be telling and reminding ourselves each day whether you aspire to be a teacher, leader, consoler, mentor, etc. Whether you think about this or not, there is always someone watching even when you think there's not maybe they are observing you (trying to pick up your body language), or because they look up to you.

The moral of the story is, there is influence in who you are and what you do, and everything you do matters. And people won't remember what you did sometimes, **but they will remember how you and it made them feel** because you've influenced them. Now you may be wondering, now that you're aware of how you've influenced you may want to make a difference in how you present yourself.

And here is the good news about that, you can use your words, your position, and your platform for good. In James, it tells us that there is Life and death in the tongue meaning that whatever comes out of our mouths either speaking life and encouraging others or speaking death and bringing others down, How do you use your words?

For your platform, how are you using your social media? Are you using it in a way that leads others astray? Or are you using it to be your authentic self and uplift others? You have the chance to change minds, make people's days, and be authentic, now will you is the question?

Here are some steps you can take to be more conscious

about your influence.

- Simply act like you're on reality tv and that people are filming you (you'll definitely be more conscious)
- Seek to make a better influence where you are right now, whether that's at school, in the community, or your inner circle (friends, family, teammates)
- Thinking before you talk, sometimes it's easy to get caught up in your feelings but thinking before we speak can help us be more aware of those around us
- Make good first impressions, you never know who's around, and when you're conscious it can work out for your benefit

GUIDE PUT TO ACTION

VERSE TO MEMORIZE:

"Let no one despite you for your youth but set the believers an example in speech. In conduct, in love, in faith, in purity."

Timothy 4:12

ACTION:

+ Choose one person in your life younger than you and work on influencing them for the good (Speaking life into her, showing her tips & tricks with the sport she is in, bible studies, etc.)

MY TIP TO YOU:

+ Don't let others, insecurities stop you from influencing others for the good.

APPLICATION:

+ Start a journal and journal each day to see how far you have come
+ Write down day or this week everything you did in relation of interacting with others & then ask yourself if you are proud of the way you have influenced.

Last thoughts:

What do you want to be remembered for.
Once you have identified that, start now.

Chapter 5

Faith

"Faith is to believe in what we do not see, and the reward of this faith is to see what we believe."

—AUGUSTINE

*F**aith,*** The thing about faith is that it's so important and I wish it was talked about more, so we are going there. And again, as your big sister I'm obligated to tell you that as I'm writing this, I'm praying that you'll not only discover faith in yourself but also faith in your relationships, your future, and God. The definition *of faith is complete trust or confidence in someone or something*.

Okay so now let that definition sink in complete trust or confidence, and at times that may be hard because were human and were not always going to be 100% full of faith at all times but acknowledging faith and clinging on to faith will help us get through this hard life. I'm going to be talking about Faith in three categories: Life, Yourself, and God.

FAITH IN GOD

Faith in God, before I continue let me preference that just because you may have had a bad experience with religion doesn't mean that God himself is bad, people will always fail us, but God won't. So let me tell you a story from my life, from since I could remember I was I guess what they call boy crazy. I had this one crush in middle school let's call him Liam and I told everyone I liked him because I was so fascinated with him, oh and there let's call him Jacob and I chased him for like two years, oh and yup the hockey player let's call him Ryan I had the biggest crush on him, and he totally played me.

The moral of the story is I put my faith and trust and honestly all my happiness and worth in if a guy liked me or not. And, with learning more about God and who He is, I know my identity isn't guys but in Christ himself and that only God alone can satisfy the parts of me that feels empty. And, after learning more about God, as even writing this part of the book right now I turned in my bible heading to Ephesians and came across this verse which almost had me in tears. In Jonah 4:2, "didn't I say before I left home that you would do this Lord? This is why I ran away to Tarshish! I knew that you are a merciful and compassionate God, slow to get angry and filled with unfailing love. You are eager to turn back from destroying people." This is the God I get to serve and the God who will change your life if you ask, He is so worth it, and He can completely change your life and transform you if you let Him. (See Bonus Content if you are interested in learning more)

FAITH IN LIFE

Honestly, Sister life is hard but it's so worth it, let me say it again life is hard but so worth it. From the moment we are born, pain will eventually hit us all whether it's emotionally, physically, or spiritually. But no matter what, do not give up you are loved, you are worth it, and you matter. And, in life, we go through hard circumstances, we can remember that there's a God who is always with us, and not only that, but the storm will pass, so have faith in that.

Now what does having faith in life even mean exactly? Having faith in life means that despite what pain or hard circumstances we go through in life we know that the pain is temporary and that we will make it through, and good things are coming. Also, it's having faith that after you have gone through things, that you believe that you still deserve good things.

FAITH IN YOURSELF

You may wonder how you can have faith in yourself after all of the things you've been through? Like Dazejah you don't know all the situations I stayed in though I knew I deserved better, and all the times I made decisions that I wished I didn't. Well even after all that, I still have good news for you. Despite what decisions you made or didn't make is in the past. And it will remain the past and there's nothing you can do about it besides forgive and move on. So, love give yourself grace and have faith that you can do the impossible.

And I know for some hearing that is hard, but I wanted to share a valuable statement, that may help: **"It is hard to know your worth if you don't even know yourself."** You may be thinking that you already know your worth and yourself and if you do, I'm so happy for you. But for the rest of us when you have faith in yourself, you have faith in your worth (you know who you are, which leads you knowing yourself more and loving.) So, for all my girlies who don't know themselves or are still in the process of learning, here are some tips.

- Learn about where you came from, who your ancestors were, about your family tree and your bloodline's history
- Try new hobbies and activities to see what you like and don't like to
- Learn what you will and will not allow in a future guy (yellow flags, green flags, red flags)
- Collect your story and heal from anything that's preventing you from being the person you are meant to be

GUIDE PUT TO ACTION

VERSE TO MEMORIZE:

"Blessed are they that have not seen, and yet believed."

John 20:29

ACTION:

+ Work on making Faith a priority in statement in your life by implicating all the areas of faith. Go to church, trust yourself to make a hard decision, Write down your dreams and chase them, etc.

MY TIP TO YOU:

+ Having faith isn't always going to be easy but it is necessary so don't give up.

APPLICATION:

+ Start a journal and journal each day to see how far you have come
+ Choose on thing you learned in this chapter and apply it to your life this week

Last thoughts:

*If they don't try, you wont ever know
so try this faith thing its worth it I promise.*

Chapter 6

Health

"Health is the Greatest Possession"

—LAZOI

*H*ealth is more than just having a good body and feeling good. Heath is everything it determines the course of our lives. If you are in bad health physically that may lead to life threatening conditions. If our Mental Health isn't in good condition, it will affect our lives and our actions.

Our health affects everything from our thoughts to how we function with others. If our mental health is bad then, we may project that onto others and it may manifest itself as a bad mood, depression, or even gossip due to low self-esteem. I will be discussing different types of Health: Physical Health, Emotional Health, and Spiritual Health in this Chapter.

MENTAL HEALTH

Let's get into it. First, we will be talking about Mental Health. Did you know that according to the World Health Organization, about 1 in 7 Adolescents experiences some type of Mental Disorder? And Depression and Anxiety are the leading causes of Illnesses among teens?

Y'all, we need to address this, because Mental Health is so important and although it is being talked about more, which is great.

Some Ways that we can improve our Mental Health so our Health can improve as well.

- **Journaling each day** our thoughts and how we're feeling (because our emotions are valid)
- **Talking to someone you trust** such as a close friend or family member about how you are truly doing
- **Grounding ourselves in truth** such as getting into the Bible and speaking affirmations & truth over ourselves
- **Consider Therapy,** I'm so passionate about it, it works and is so beneficial

PHYSICAL HEALTH

Physical Health as you already know it is super important, but do you know why? Physical Health is so important for many reasons, One being that Science confirms that working out our bodies boosts Serotonin. And Serotonin improves your mood and when our mood improves it not only improves our Physical Health because we feel good but also improves our Mental Health because it lowers Depression.

Some Ways to Improve Physical Health is by:

- Moving our bodies at least 20 minutes each day
- Hot Girl Walks (with a Podcast or some jams on)
- Doing Pilates at least twice a week (has amazing benefits for overall health)

EMOTIONAL HEALTH

Emotional Health by definition is *a person's ability to accept and manage feelings through challenge and change.* And Emotional Health is so important because we will all suffer and face hardships sometime in our lives. And we have to be able to acknowledge the feelings that we are facing and be able to manage them appropriately. And I wanted to emphasize that what one person's hardship may be considered huge to one, but to another it may deemed as small and temporary. Now it is important to remember is that everyone's feelings in whatever situation they may face are valid and important. And if we see another sister facing a hardship, we should walk alongside her.

Emotional Health is important because it is centered around how we interact and deal with life flows from it. How we socially interact with others, How we deal with relationships, and even How we cope when times get hard.

Now scientifically, here are some ways to improve your Emotional Health:

- Seek and nurture healthy relationships
- Managing our stress efficiently

- Coping with our Emotions appropriately
- Improving your Self-Awareness

SPIRITUAL HEALTH

Spiritual Health is all about connecting with God, yourself, others, and Nature. And I wanted to make sure to include this because one thing I don't see talked about enough is the fact that Spiritual Health can and will affect all of the other forms of health. An example is that The Bible talks about renewing the mind with thoughts above, and we can see that is we aren't striving to constantly be renewing our minds that our Mental Health will be affected one way or another. And how Physically if we aren't treating our bodies as temples then our Physical Health and Spiritual Heath will heap the effects.

Some ways to improve your Spiritual Health:

- Start a prayer journal and talk to God daily through it
- Connect with a church and get involved in small groups
- Get connected in nature

Lastly, what I want you to take from this chapter is the importance of health in all types. As I emphasized before, Physical Health is so important for our bodies, because we feel good about ourselves, and our bodies are function properly.

And Mental Health is SOOO important and I'm happy it is being talked about more but it's something that needs to be continuously talked about. It's all Mental, it's all in the mind, and I'll let you in on a secret if you want to change your thought process. The Bible says that all things we do flow from the heart, and the truth is what is in our heart is what we think about and that eventually becomes what we do. An example would be if we have been told lies about ourselves by a bully, parent, or ex-friends then we may subconsciously think maybe they are right. And if we don't believe we are good enough in our hearts, then we will treat ourselves as if we aren't good enough.

So, if you want to become the girl you are meant to be start with Health. Start to crack down on the lies that you built your foundation on and talk about it and learn to build a new foundation on truth. And for our Physical Health, if we want to improve our body, we need to do it out of love for ourselves and not hate for ourselves.

Repeat this after me, *"I love myself enough to make a change and I'm not doing this because I hate myself."*

GUIDE PUT TO ACTION

VERSE TO MEMORIZE:

"So whatever you eat or drink or whatever you do, do it all for the glory of God."

1 Corinthians 10:31

ACTION:

+ Improve your health in all the aspects today by changing one thing. (EX. Journal. Workout. Church. Therpay. Mediate)

MY TIP TO YOU:

+ Seek help or guidance when needed we don't have to be perfect in all of these, but we should be prioritizing if you need support get some!!

APPLICATION:

+ Start a journal and journal each day to see how far you have come
+ Pick one specific form of health and focus on improving it this month

Last thoughts:

Health is one of our greatest gifts, so let's nurture her!!

Chapter 7

Confidence

*"With confidence, you have won before
you have started."*

—MARCUS GARVEY

Fake it until you make it. How many times have you heard that saying? I know I've heard it so many times and I want to talk about it. Confidence is so critical to have especially as a woman, continuously knowing your worth and your value is so important. Just knowing you were created for a purpose and were chosen to be alive in this generation and this moment is so beautiful to think about.

And One Thing that I believe is so infuriating to think about is how when we were younger, we didn't care what people thought of us and now as teens we have become so self-conscious. I just wonder how we as women have gotten here? Is it because we over time became people pleasers? Is it because don't know our worth? Is it because that boy rejected us? Whatever the reason may be now I believe that's something we're putting an end to now. Confidence in yourself means we love and accept ourselves as who we are flaws and all and we love us, despite our mistakes. Maybe you went through a path in your life where you felt like you've hit rock bottom and lost the confidence and hope in yourself but listen to what I'm about to say.

One of my favorite sayings said by the iconic Steve Harvey is, *"What other people think about you is none of your business."* Now let me dive down into that more, what others think is none of our business. That has power in it, other's thoughts, actions, and words toward you, aren't actually about you. We need to change our narrative and thought process about that.

Someone doesn't like us? Our response is we don't care. Someone doesn't like that outfit? Too bad. Someone is spreading rumors? Are they that insecure? Changing the way respond to it is critical but in reality, it's not our business to respond to their insecurities. It's our job to do the things as women that make us feel confident that matter. So, wear that dress to the bookstore and live out your dreams. So, bake cookies at 2 am and post all about it on your insta story. And even wear those iconic throwback outfits to class because it is your style and live to the fullest because in the end being confident is so important for our Mental, Physical, and Spiritual Health.

MENTALLY

How does mental health and confidence correlate, you may ask? The correlation is simple if you feel good about yourself, you will think good of yourself, and it will show. If you don't feel good about yourself, you will think negatively of yourself, it will show. If you want to improve your confidence, you have to improve the way you think mentally, and change the way you view yourself. Do you need to forgive yourself? Do you need to learn more about yourself? Do you need to speak to yourself kinder? Figure out whatever that may be and then do it, and it's a daily practice and it won't happen overnight. **Some first steps can be**

- **Go in front of your mirror** each day and say good things about yourself (''I'm beautiful', 'I'm loved', 'I'm chosen.'')
- **Seek the root** of why you're thinking negatively about yourself (is it because of what someone said? What people spoke
- over you, that they shouldn't have? Is it because of your past?
- **Give yourself the love you wish you had** (go on self-dates, tell yourself you love yourself, write down your negative thoughts and next to it write down the truth)

PHYSICALLY

If you feel good, you'll feel confident. How can you physically feel good about yourself? You may ask? Maybe it's going on a run, maybe it is getting 8 hours of sleep, or maybe it is working out to fit into that dress you've been dreaming of. The truth is when you work out, your body releases chemicals that improve your mood, and when your mood is improved, so is your well-being. So, if you want to improve your confidence

Physically, you could:

- Workout, (if you're new you can start 2 days a week and then gradually move up)

- Eat more nutritious foods, so you feel better
- Get 8-9 hours of sleep (you will feel better, and have more energy)

SPIRITUALLY

If you would like to feel more confident spiritually, then you can start by simply learning more about God and asking the hard questions. You don't know unless you ask, and The Bible states, ''For everyone who asks, receives, Everyone who seeks, finds. And to everyone who knocks the door will be opened. '' (Matthew 7:8). And there is something in all of us that we crave that no guy, no parent, or friend can fill only God and when we learn more about him and call upon his name, He can fill what we've been looking for.

Lastly, some first steps can be:

- Getting into the Word each day
- Listening to Worship Music
- Praying each Morning and Night

And honestly, Confidence is hard because we go through things in our lives that affect our confidence in one way or another. Whether from trauma during childhood or that bully from middle school or that guy who simply chose another girl over you. And despite all of that as your big sis I'm here to tell you we don't have to live in the victim mentality. Whatever someone did to you to shatter your confidence and self-worth we don't have to allow them to have that full victory over you.

Let me explain that guy who played you as a bet, has nothing on you now, as far as I remember Jesus defeated any hold over us 2,000 years ago on the cross. So, allow your past and all the messy parts of your story become something broken to something beautiful. Don't allow anyone from your past to keep you in a hold, that you have been freed from. Now if God woke you up today, He is not done with you, so grow your Self-Worth because you are fearfully and wonderfully made, have a big purpose, and go grow to become the girl you're meant to be.

GUIDE PUT TO ACTION

VERSE TO MEMORIZE:

''So we say with confidence, 'The Lord is my helper; I will not be afraid. What can mere mortals do to me."

Hebrews 13:6

ACTION:

+ DO something out of the ordinary for you today (This will boast your confidence)

MY TIP TO YOU:

+ BE CONFIDENT, because people will know if you aren't.

APPLICATION:

+ Start a journal and journal each day to see how far you have come
+ Pick oen of the areas of confidence and work on being more confident in these areas.

Last thoughts:

*Being confident wont happen over night but it is a choice &
each day you will get once step closer!!*

Chapter 8

Sisterly Advice

"A Sister is a friend you don't have to
avoid the truth with."

—JOY MCCULLOUGH

This was my favorite chapter to write besides the second chapter. Today I will be talking about the importance of advice and guidance from another older wiser girl. I believe that having someone who will speak life to you, encourage you, and point you to truth is so important and that is why I am here.

FIND GOOD COMMUNITY

And the biggest advice I can give you about community is simply finding someone who will ride with you on this crazy thing called life. You want a friend who's going to be like you cry, I cry, you are happy, I'm happy alongside you, you need someone to vent to, I'm the person you can vent to. We need someone who can be that for us whether it's a big sister, mentor, or best friend. We all need someone and as I'm writing this, I hope my words inspire you.

I also can advise you to get involved as much as you can in sports and activities. As I'm writing this, I'm finishing my senior year of high school and I realized that even though I joined a sport within my senior year. I missed out on so many opportunities to join other sports and activities that could have helped me grew so much.

As I watch videos on finding community in college and have talked to some people, One of the biggest pieces of advice they have given was about talking to any and everyone. Now, let me rephrase I'm not saying go up to creepy people and talk to them I'm saying, if there's someone in your class that seems nice, talk to them.

TALK TO PEOPLE YOU DON'T KNOW

If you're in line next to someone in the Sephora line, compliment them, One of my favorite quotes I've heard is *you haven't met all of the people who are going to love you yet,* so if you're sitting here thinking about how you haven't met your people yet, or sad because you haven't met the one, or maybe upset because you don't feel you can be your genuine self with the people in your life, remember that quote.

BE YOURSELF

Another sisterly piece of advice I can give you is to be your authentic self, all the way, all in. And those who truly care about you will love you for your authentic self. Your authentic self your sarcasm (not mean ones lol), the fact that you talk too much about random things, and the fact that you love singing randomly (New Girl reference haha). or me my genuine authentic self is if you truly get to know me, I won't shut up I love talking and having raw genuine conversations, me being a leader, and the fact I seek opportunities to be in charge or help when needed, the fact that if you are crying, I will be crying as well, and the fact that if my song comes on in the car, I will be singing my tail off, do you know why?

Well because that's me and I won't change me, just because someone doesn't like it. And I advise you to do the same if someone doesn't like the way you laugh or the fact that you do you, forget them being you is important because that's how we connect with others who are like us, we are ourselves and those who will unconditionally love that will show up.

GUARD YOUR HEART

Also, it's important to know and truly know that not everyone has your best interest at heart, some people aren't meant to see your true vulnerable raw self emotionally and physically because not everyone is meant for you. **Proverbs 4:23 says,'"Guard your heart above all else for it determines the course of your life."** Whether you follow or believe the Bible or not this verse is crucial and important, guarding our heart against that boy, that one night stand, that heartbreak is crucial and important because it can spare us tears, and pain, and as your big sister from a distance, I'm sharing this because I care. Some people will be deceitful and not have true intentions when speaking and encountering you.

WAIT FOR THE ONE

My biggest advice is to wait for a guy who waits for you, a guy whose eyes light up when he sees you, a guy who prays for you that's the type of guy you want sis. And remember a guy who pressures you isn't the guy for you, one of my favorite songs is Make Him Wait by Abby Anderson, **she says** *"make him wait by the phone, at the door to meet your dad, before that first kiss, he's got to hold your hand."*

I say that as I'm writing this chapter right now, those lyrics gave me the courage to now make that a boundary that I uphold as a standard in my future relationships with a guy, because I value them, and if he values me, he'll value that too! To conclude, love yourself enough to wait and to guard your heart against preventable heartbreak.

Having a boyfriend is fun. Having someone who you can spend lots of time with and love on is fun too. But, if we long for it too much, we can make it an idol and maybe even settle when we should have waited.

Now onto the raw piece of advice, I can give you first to not be afraid to talk to someone new and go up to them. And, before you put the book down after I just said that, listen to the advice I'm about to give. Now as I'm writing this part of the chapter, I'm a college freshman and at college and one thing I've realized more than anything is that **how you row is how you grow.** Let me elaborate on how you put yourself out their matters, if you go up to people and introduce yourself to people, which may be outside of your comfort zone, you will grow.

If you show up with confidence when meeting new people, then you'll automatically grow because you're rowing towards the path of success (sis you're making connections). And that's the type of person you want to aim to be as you get older and go through life.

NEVER PURSE A GUY

Yes, sis you heard me never chase a guy I know that may be hard because you may like this guy and want to talk to him all day, every day. But a quote I want you to hear and reflect on is, ''If you pursued, you would have never known if he would have pursued first.'' WOAHHH sis as I just wrote that, it still hits me every time. If you always texted him, made plans with him first, and called him you would have never known if he would have done it first.

I want to tell you a story. There was this guy that I followed on Instagram, who also goes to my school, and oh girl when I tell you he was perfect, he was perfect (well almost). He and I liked similar music, same beliefs, both passionate, and he liked my stories the only con was that he took forever to respond like days, but he was active.

Long story short, I pursued him, but he didn't pursue me, and I would have never known if he would have made a move if I wouldn't hadn't done so first. So sister, let him pursue and make the first move and if you're interested and he's good for you, reciprocate it.

YOU DON'T KNOW, UNLESS YOU TRY

It says in Psalms 39:4, *"Lord, remind me how brief my time on earth will be. Remind me that my days are numbered- how fleeting my life is."* From the moment we were born, we all have a certain that we will be here on earth, and we should make sure that we use our days wisely but also make the most of each day. I'm not talking about partying but simply exploring the world, meeting new people, and leaving a good mark on the world.

GUIDE PUT TO ACTION

VERSE TO MEMORIZE:

"Be wise in the way you act toward outsiders; make the most of every opportunity. Let your conversation be always full of grace, seasoned with salt, so that you may know how to answer everyone."

Colossians 4:5-6

ACTION:

+ Pick an area I mentioned and put action towards upholding that (Ex. Not pursing a guy but clearly making it known that you are interested.)

MY TIP TO YOU:

+ Take my advice or another women's advice who has been through this, because it can prevent you from it

APPLICATION:

+ Start a journal and journal each day to see how far you have come
+ Do something that you have never tried that you felt held back from doing

Last thoughts:

Always be you and do what is best for you.

Chapter 9

Choose Your Battle

*"The Artist is nothing without the gift,
but the gift is nothing without work."*

—EMILE ZOLA

C hoose your battle. You have gifts that people don't have that could change the world but are you willing to is the question? There are so many injustices in this world and by using your skills & talents alongside identifying those passions, things will shift.

One of my favorite quotes by Rihanna is when she was talking after receiving an award. She said, **"It's a women's problem, it's a black people problem, it's a poor people problem, and if there's anything that I've learned it's that we can only fix this world together, We can't do it divided I can't emphasize that enough."**

I believe that's the mentality that we have to have when approaching current issues and struggles of life. And preach to everyone that you don't have to do it alone and that there are other people there that want to fight that battle alongside you.

And it's not just a "your problem", it's our problem, because if there's anything I want you to take with you from reading this book. It is this, you want and need people who are going to ride with you through the mud, shine, rain, storm, and beyond. We want and need people who are in our lives who are like, "you jump, I jump" because if they truly care and you are struggling it is our problem until the outcome will become your solution.

Another important thing when choosing your skill is to think of all of the things that are important topics to you that drive you to want change.

Some Social Issues that aren't as talked about as much but are critical for change can range from:

- Children in foster care systems/ orphanages
- Advocating towards teen mothers (and not shamming)
- Fighting for refugees
- At risk Children & their futures
- Prison Reform

And I believe that this generation can be the change because we all have things that ignite our souls to want to make a change.

Some of my favorite Organizations that fight these Social Issues are:
- The Arise Box (helps Women Trafficking Victims)
- The Love Box (helps Mothers with unplanned pregnancies with a message of hope)
- Let Them Live (donates money to mothers in need)

And maybe you're not sure of passions you have that encourage you to want to fight for change and that's okay. I recommend trying out different ones, start by volunteering at each one to help you narrow down.

Some ideas for Organizations to dip your foot in are

- Volunteering at Rehibition Center for animals
- Volunteering at Pregnancy Resource center to help mothers who feel hopeless
- Volunteering at Homeless Shelter to help families
- Volunteering for Ocean Clean Ups around the world and help save the planet
- Volunteering at the hospital and giving hope and encouragement to children or elderly who are sick

But remember whatever that you do, Remember that no opportunity is one that is wasted so even after all of that, you still don't know that is okay at least you made a difference.

But if you're reading this and if have a fire for wanting to make a change, here's some advice: not everyone is going to agree with what you're doing no matter how good of a cause it may be, you have to develop the courage to do it anyways.

Some little ways that make a big difference

- Writing to your local legislation to push for them to advocate for problems you're passionate about
- Donate some money to organizations that you're passionate about
- Write Christmas cards for your local nursing home, veterans, or homeless shelter
- Host a prayer night with friends to pray for a Social Issue
- Make Blessing Bags with friends or family and give them to the homeless
- Start doing some research and informing people around you about them
- Buy a Christmas present and give it to a single mother that you know struggling

And don't forget that it is so important to choose your battles, we can have a lot of passions, but we don't have to fight for every single one because enough people are fighting the ones you're not. And learn more about you and what you are passionate about and what your strengths are. Why you may ask? because you are stuck with you for the rest of your life and discovering who you are and the skills, gifts, and passions God gave you have power.

Here are some questions you can ask yourself when it comes to discovering your passion and skills:

- What's your dream job or career that you are passionate about?
- What's something you're good at naturally? Singing? Art? Public Speaking?
- What's that one thing that's in your heart that you just can't explain, there's just something about it?

And never forget that you are so worth it and so is your life and there is no one like you on here. You have unique talents and gifts that you can change the world for the better.

GUIDE PUT TO ACTION

VERSE TO MEMORIZE:

"Each of you should use whatever gift you have received to serve others, as faithful stewards of Gods Grace in its various forms."

1 Peter 4:10

ACTION:

+ Get involved we were called to make a difference in this world, so go make a difference!!

MY TIP TO YOU:

+ Don't overwhelm yourself once you get involved and active when using your gifts, make sure to take time to rest.

APPLICATION:

+ Start a journal and journal each day to see how far you have come
+ Start your Volunteer & Activism Journey

Last thoughts:

It is okay if others don't like the battles, you choose or the way you use your gift, Be you regardless.

Chapter 10

For the Heartbroken, asking Will I Ever Move On?

"In three words I can sum up everything I learned in life: It goes on."

—ROBERT FROST

I *have been heartbroken.* I have had my heart crushed by a boy I wanted to marry one day. I have had my heart broken when that friend broke my trust. I have had my heart broken when something I worked so hard for, was taken away from me. And honesty heartbreak sucks. Who broke your heart? That situationship? Or Maybe that one you didn't even date? Your boyfriend of 2 years? Your own friends?

I don't know who it was or what happened but let me say this to you. Sometimes heartbreak deserves all the slander it gets because it hurt us more than we can image. And sometimes Heartbreak can be one of the best things that could have happened to us. Yes, I said it, What if that boy who you didn't date rejected you actually was for good? Do you ever just think that it didn't work out because there was someone better?

One of my favorite sayings I have ever heard is *"You're not stuck because you can't, you're stuck because you won't."* And now that you have heard that let me elaborate on what I just said, but first let me tell you a story. It started when I met this guy and we worked together, and we have known each other for a few months. But it was summer this time and we were talking more, and I tried to pursue a friendship when this guy, and then you may have guessed what came next, what typically happens,

I ended up having feelings for this guy and he didn't feel the same. And what was the worst part, was in the process of trying to get him to like me or even be interested in me, I lost a piece of myself while doing it, I did what a girl should never do, chase a guy, especially one who's not interested. I would even post extra on social media just so he would see it, I would wear more makeup so he would see it, and I even did the classic girl hack of leaving him on delivered extra-long, just so he would want to chase me. And what ended up happening in the end is he chose someone else than me and he didn't like me back, to him I wasn't worthy.

What I learned from that chapter of my life is that as the quote says I let myself be sad and not move on not because I couldn't but because I no longer allowed the hold, he had over me of what could have been. And what was hard about that was I preached over and over about not letting a guy get to you and loving yourself even to my friends at the time and I didn't even take my own advice. Now after that, I've moved on, I'm living and learned that if a guy respects you, he will not say rude things to you after you guys are over. He will not leave you wondering what you guys are. He will not ignore your presence but instead purse respectfully. That is not love, and that is not respect, that is why it's so important to choose a guy who respects and treats you the way you deserve.

Let me also emphasize and say that not all guys are like that when it comes to the ending of whatever was there. And I cannot read your mind, but I'm going to give one reason, might be in your heart is because you think of what could have been if things did not end or what you could have done instead. And I'm here to tell you that living in the what-ifs is one of the most dangerous mindsets and changing your thoughts about it is the key to healing.

I believe that where you are is where you as supposed to be, right now and that relationships and things may happen for you to learn a lesson. That relationship taught you how important trust is, maybe it even taught you what you want and need in a future relationship. And Heartbreak is only temporary, and the pain is also temporary, and it may feel in the moment like you won't ever get over it, but I'm telling you, will.

Now let's talk about ways to heal from the pain:

- Allow yourself to feel the hurt (crying is 1000% okay!!)
- Unfriend, Unsee, and Uncare
- **Unfriend** him on social media
- **Unsee** him every day, do not make plans to see each other
- **Uncare** about what he's doing in his everyday life after the relationship ended (especially if he was toxic, do not dwell)

Something I can highly recommend doing is using the 3 U's when healing and moving on from a guy.

First, **Unfriend** him on social media at least for right now what he is doing with his life after us is no longer our concern. The next is **Unsee** him, do not make plans for an effort to try and see him to ''just talk'' about what's going on in your life or the classic excuse ''do you have the notes we took'' or ''what Did I miss in class'', ask someone else. Lastly, **Uncare** about him, don't care about if he has a new girlfriend or if he got accepted into that college, focus on bringing that love and care towards yourself.

Remember what's meant for you, will be yours in due time if it's meant to happen; having that said and done if you guys are meant to be together God will bring you guys back together if that's a part of his will. In the back of the book, I'll talk more about the 3 U's if you want additional information!

MOVING ON

Moving on, why is it so hard, why is tough to get over our first love? That crush we had for 5 years? Oh, and that Situationship, why can't I get over him? And don't even get me started on that best friend who is no longer our best friend? These are all examples of things that are hard to move on from and forget like this isn't supposed to be easy right? Here's the truth, moving on is so hard but honestly, it's so it's crucial for us to be where we're not only supposed to be but also for what's to come.

So sister, you will go through some form of heartbreak again, and it will hurt and it won't be fun but don't give up on love because of your past. Always be open to love because you deserve to be loved.

GUIDE PUT TO ACTION

VERSE TO MEMORIZE:

"The Lord is close to the brokenhearted, he rescues those whose spirits are crushed."

Psalms 34:18

ACTION:

+ Write down all your past hurts and heartbreak and then do something about it. Do you to talk through it? Let out your feelings in a healthy way? Go do it!!

MY TIP TO YOU:

+ One thing I like to do when experiencing heart break is writing a letter to that person and saying everything, I wish I could have said and last thoughts. (It works every time)

APPLICATION:

+ Start a journal and journal each day to see how far you have come
+ Apply what you learned through this chapter and highlight what stood out to you & so some reflection with it.

Last thoughts:

It's okay to grieve and make you sure you have time to process but don't go through it alone, especially in cases of death of someone close to you or a messy breakup.

Conclusion

Here is the truth, this life isn't easy, and we are not guaranteed to have a pain, trial-free life although that would be great, we aren't promised that. And maybe even after reading this book you may still feel discouraged and be like, yes, I see where you are coming from, but my situation hasn't changed, I'm still stuck in a cycle, my heart is still broken, and so on. But I wanted to remind you that redeems, be forever, and you don't have to stay stuck if I could have you take anything from this book it would be two things: Jesus still redeems and We can choose how we live our life, PERIOD. Jesus can redeem you and your situation, one thing I know about him is that if he did it in the past, he will do it again whether it is how we think it should be or if it's How he knows it will be. And we can choose how we live our lives, and I know that is such a general statement that we hear all the time, but it is so TRUE AND THAT'S WHAT I SAID IT. If you are not happy about your situation change it, if you don't like your job and you are burned out, Just Leave even if it takes you some time, if your friend group is toxic, Just Leave even if you'll be alone for some time, but God will provide new friends if your boyfriend is mistreating you just break up with him (if it is an abusive relationship, refer to back for hotlines), we aren't staying were we aren't getting what we deserve. So anyways this is my conclusion, you are only on this Earth once, so do everything you want to do, if you want to start a small business GO DO IT (and text me so I can buy something from you), if you want to go backpacking in Europe, GO DO IT (His Creation is beautiful), maybe you want to start a podcast but nervous about what people may think about you, GO DO IT ANYWAYS (our life do not revolve around the opinions of others). So, bestie, go write that book, release that song, or go kiss that boy, whatever it is, you only have this one life, so go live it.

ACKNOWLEDGMENTS

WOW, My Book is finally here, My dream of inspiring young women has finally come true. And besides all my hard work that went unto this process, I couldn't be more grateful for all those who helped make this come true.

Blair Parke who helped edit my book
Kathy Lee who helped create this beautiful layout for my book

WANT MORE?

If you want more content like this, I'd love to have you!! Here are some ways to keep up with me and what is to come. You can follow me on Social Media Platforms, follow my Blog where I post weekly, and stay updated because there will be a Second Book coming with more content and to come will be merch with encouraging bible verses, quotes, and symbols to have you wear to rock alongside the book.

Blog: *Let's Talk About It*
(Can be found at www.Dazejahmae.com)

Instagram: @DazejahMae

TikTok: @Worththetalk

BONUS CONTENT

Hey Loves, I created some bonus content on the next pages that will help you after you read this book. This content includes how to get saved, mini blog posts to help you, bucket lists, and so much more. You girls are so loved, and I hope and pray that you feel more equipped to combat the lies that you are stuck, alone, and not worthy. You are CAPABLE, You are WORTH IT, and You are CHOSEN. Enjoy the content.

XOXO,
Dazejah Mae

HOTLINES
What's all the Tea?

I wanted to include hotlines to this book because I understand that we as women aren't always okay. We may go through seasons of depression, insecurity about how we look, or face situations we couldn't have imagined. So that is why I created this, you can always have it with you whenever you need it, in case someone you may know will need it, or in case you want to share it with another girl who is struggling. This is for you; YOU ARE LOVED and so AMAZING.

HOTLINES

National Suicide Hotline:
1-800-SUICIDE (784-2433) + 988

National Domestic Abuse+ Violence Hotline:
1- 800-799- SAFE (7233)

National Eating Disorder Hotline:
1-(800) 931-2237

National Self Abuse Hotline:
1-800-DONT-CUT

National Consoling Hotline:
1-800-HIT-HOME

National Trafficking Healing Hotline:
1-888-373-7888

National Sexual Assault Hotline:
1-800-656-HOPE (4673)

National Crisis Pregnancy Hotline:
1-800-67-BABY-6
(260) 200-3789

MINI POSTS

Yes, I obviously had to include those because I am a blogger. These are short mini posts about three topics I believe relate to the book and what you can be reminded and encouraged of even after you have read the book.

HOW TO BECOME SAVED?

(MINI POST)

I wanted to include a reference to salvation in the end just in case you are interested.

So, the Gospel:

We were born into a perfect world and then humans sinned, and the world became sinful. And with sin comes death, abuse, disaster, and pain. And because we are imperfect and sinful, we need someone perfect to contrast everything we aren't and save us. Luckily for us there is one. And His name is Jesus, He entered this world a little over 2000 years ago. He was born from a women named Mary and lived and started his ministry spreading the Good News, performing miracles & Healing. He than was hated for what he preached and did and was sentenced to death on the cross by the people. He died on the cross and was resurrected three days later. Spoiler Alert they still haven't found this body. And the Good News is He paid the price and it is still paid, and we are redeemed if we believe in him and admit we are sinners. Oh, and I did I mention He still heals? If you want to accept him into your heart, you can pray something like this.

"Dear God, I am sitting here before you now acknowledging that I have sinned and am a sinner and that you are God and God alone, I am asking you to forgive me for my sins and wrong doings and come into my heart and be my Lord. I believe your son died on the cross and rose and I want him to mold me to be more like him. Amen"

(First off if you said something like this Congratulations! But I want to remind you that Saying those won't save you if you don't work towards following him now and by believing what you said.)

Next Steps:
- Buying a Bible
- Getting involved in a Church
- Finding an older woman to mentor and disciple you

HOW TO GET OVER A GUY

(MINI POST)

Yes, in case you were wondering, I'm a certified love expert, so let's get into it. Getting over a guy is really hard, and then on top of that, you have different types of getting over a guy. Like, the guy you didn't date, your crush, that situationship. Your ex-boyfriend. And despite all of that it can still we tricky. But here's something I heard a wise women say she said that she loses feelings for a guy simply from the sense that he has horrible taste because he missed out on a girl like her. And then she went on to say that we have to stop giving guys the all the power in the situation and realize our worth and I AGREE.

We so often don't even like the guy we like the idea of him, we fall for his potential. So, honesty this maybe should be how to get over a guy you like but the potential of the guy. So how you get over a guy you may ask? You have to reflect on what you like about him and actually reflect because you may discover it wasn't him you liked but you formed an attachment to him or how he simply wasn't even a good guy for you.

THINGS TO COME

(MINI POST)

Wow the time has come, we are at the end of the book. But here's the Good News, this isn't the end. After you finishing reading every page, the book might be done but your life isn't. As I mentioned in a previous chapter, you will go through triumphs and trials but despite all of that there are still things to come. You still have great things to look forward to. The day you graduate College. Your Wedding day. Your first Flight. Meeting your best friend. Your first child. And I did forget to say, Meeting all the people who will get to meet and love you?

There is so much to look forward to, despite the bad. You are going to have bad days. Get your heart broken. And be broke at some point in your life. But wouldn't you rather go through every good, bad, ugly, and beautiful thing that life has to offer and leave this Earth being able to say, I am proud I didn't give up despite it all, and that I remembered that there are things to come.

9 SELF DATE IDEAS YOU'LL FALL IN LOVE WITH

1. Barnes & Noble Date

This one is my personal favorite, just wearing my favorite outfit and going to read books and treating myself is so fun.

2. Movies Date

Put on your favorite PJ's and go to the movies and watch the movie you have been waiting months for

Take yourself on a movie date, buy that popcorn and enjoy the time alone

3. Starbucks Date

Get in your car & drive to the closest Starbucks and curl up with your favorite book or do some work on your laptop and go buy that latte

4. Dinner Date

Go to your favorite restaurant and get dressed up and treat yourself.

5. Spa Night

Take a warm bath, do face masks, listen to calming music and enjoy the relaxation

6. Shopping Spree!

Spoil yourself by going to your favorite stores and buying something new or head to the thrift stores and shop your heart away

7. Gardening Date

Head to your local store and buy some wildflowers or your favorite vegetables and go outside put on some music and enjoy being in nature & trying a new hobby

8. Go to a Concert

Head on to Ticketmaster and look up your favorite bands or artists and see when they come and buy the ticket and get dressed up, you wont regret it

Look up local concerts such as concerts in the park or at the local theater or church and then buy the ticket and get dressed up and have a great time (I saw Anne Wilson this way)

9. Go do a Beach Picnic

Head to the closest beach towards you, stop at the store and buy your favorite snacks or pack your favorite fruits and head to the beach have that fun playlist ready and bring a blanket to sit on and some books or the bible and watch the sunset or the beautiful ocean view

BUCKET LIST IDEAS YOU'LL FALL IN LOVE WITH

- Turtle Sanctuary in Palm Beach Florida

- Take a Pottery Class (Locations all around the country)

- Do Baby Goat Yoga or some sort of workout that involves goats (Various locations around the country)

- Go on a retreat that will better your life (LIFE Retreat. Wellness Retreats, etc.)

- Visit the Skopelos Island in Greece and live out your *Mamma Mia* dream

- Attend the Water Lantern Festival in Washington, DC

Hi ladies, so I did a thing. I asked some guys questions that us girls want to know. So, the next four pages will include questions that I asked a variety of guys, and what their responses are. I wanted to include this not only to give us women some insight, but also to show you that guys do think differently than us. But they are more alike us than we think, and through this we can learn to give guys grace because we are just children of God trying to figure out this crazy journey called life.

DISCLAIMER: NAMES OF THE GUYS HAVE BEEN CHANGED FOR PRIVACY REASONS.

QUESTIONS GIRLS WANT TO KNOW, AND GUYS' RESPONSES

I spilled all the tea on asking guys some questions to give some insight for us women to better understand their thinking. I hope you enjoy.

DO GUYS CARE ABOUT WHAT PEOPLE THINK ABOUT THEM?

"ONLY WHAT MY CLOSE FRIENDS THINK."
—JOHN

"DEPENDS ON THE GUY, BUT I WOULD SAY MOST OF THE TIME YES."
—BRODY

"YES"
—AROUND 40% OF THE GUYS WHO DID THIS POLL AGREED.

Q: DO YOU BELIEVE A GUY AND GIRL CAN BE JUST FRIENDS?

"YES OF COURSE."
—AROUND 70% OF GUYS SAID THEY AGREED. GUYS AND GIRLS CAN BE FRIENDS.

"YES WITH BOUNDARIES."
—AROUND 23% SAID WITH BOUNDARIES THE FRIENDSHIP WOULD WORK.

"NO NOT POSSIBLE."
—AROUND 1% DISAGREED.

Q: CAN YOU TELL IF A GIRL IS DESPERATE TO TALK TO YOU?

"YES, IT IS OBVIOUS."
—AROUND 40% OF THE GUYS SAID THAT THEY COULD TELL.

"NO."
—AROUND 30% OF THE GUYS SAID THEY COULDN'T TELL.

Q: WHAT IS THE FIRST THING YOU NOTICE ABOUT A GIRL?

"INTROVERT/EXTROVERT OR PERSONALITY."

—JAMES

"SMILE."

—ABOUT 1/4 OF THE GUYS POLLED SAID THAT SMILE AND FACE ARE AMONG THE FIRST THINGS THEY NOTICE.

"EYES."

—ABOUT 1/4 OF THE GUYS POLLED SAID THAT EYES ARE AMONG THE FIRST THINGS THEY NOTICE.

Q: DO YOU BELIEVE THAT BODY SIZE MATTERS IN A RELATIONSHIP?

"NO."

—AROUND 60% OF THE GUYS POLLED SAID THEY DON'T.

"YES BUT AS THEY MATURE, IT BECOMES LESS IMPORTANT"

—BRODY

"IT DOESN'T MATTER PER SAY, BUT GUYS WILL HAVE PREFERENCES THE SAME AS ANY PHYSICAL FEATURES."

—JUDE

Q: IF YOU LIKE A GIRL DO YOU TELL HER?

"IF THE CRUSH LAST LONGER THAN THREE WEEKS, YES."

—BRENDAN

"AS OFTEN AS I CAN."

—MICHAEL

"IF I'M ATTRACTED TO A GIRL, ILL ASK HER FOR HER NUMBER AND ASK HER OUT."

—STEPHEN

Q: IF YOU COULD GIVE ANY ADVICE TO GIRLS INSIGHT REGARDING GUYS, WHAT WOULD YOU SAY?

"GUYS DON'T HAVE A CLUE IF YOU LIKE THEM OR NOT SO IF YOU LIKE US, TELL US."

—TYLER

"BE KIND ALWAYS, SOMETIMES GIRLS HURT GUYS AND THEY DON'T KNOW."

—JUSTIN

"BE SOMEONE WORTH PURSING, HAVE A GENUINE LOVE FOR LIFE AND THE PEOPLE AROUND YOU AND MEN WILL TAKE NOTICE."

—JUDE